T0317930

PAPER
FOLDING
LEARN IN
A WEEKEND

First published in the United Kingdom in 2024
by Skittledog, an imprint of Thames & Hudson Ltd,
181A High Holborn, London WC1V 7QX

Concept and layout © Thames & Hudson 2024

Text © Kate Colin 2024

All Rights Reserved. No part of this publication may be
reproduced or transmitted in any form or by any means,
electronic or mechanical, including photocopy, recording
or any other information storage and retrieval system,
without prior permission in writing from the publisher.

British Library Cataloguing-in-Publication Data
A catalogue record for this book is available from
the British Library

ISBN 978-1-837-76045-9

Printed and bound China by C&C Offset Printing Co., Ltd

Senior Editor: Virginia Brehaut
Photographer: Charles Emerson
Designer: Masumi Briozzo
Production: Felicity Awdry

Additional photography on page 11 by Alaisdair Smith
Photography; 'Partick Bridge' print on page 11 by Libby
Walker and wallpaper on page 27 by Natascha Maksimovic

The work of other paper artists included in the book
is used with permission and the creators retain the right
to be recognized as the copyright holders.

Be the first to know about our new releases, exclusive
content and author events by visiting:

skittledog.com
thamesandhudson.com
thamesandhudsonusa.com
thamesandhudson.com.au

PAPER FOLDING
LEARN IN A WEEKEND

KATE COLIN

Skittledog

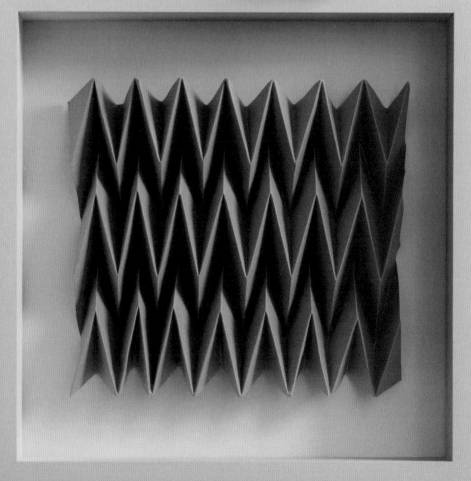

CONTENTS

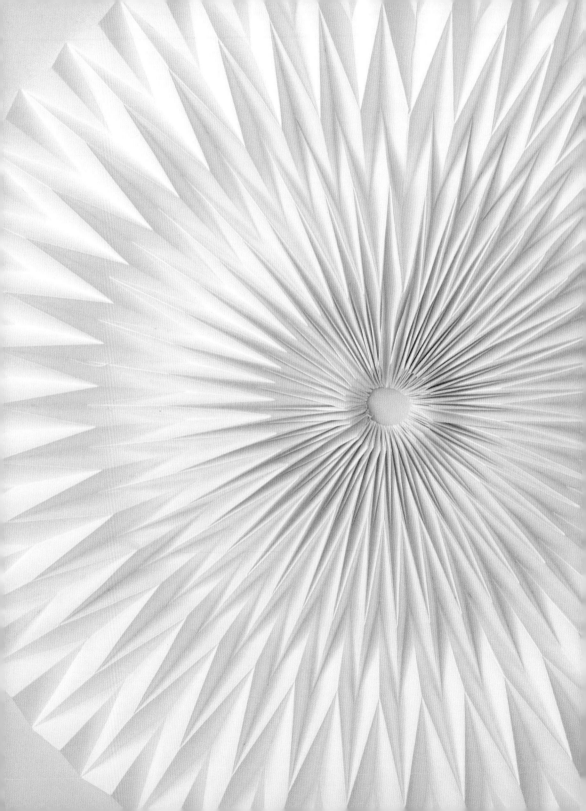

INTRODUCTION

There is nothing more wondrous than seeing a flat piece of paper become a three-dimensional form, simply through the act of folding. With the help of this book, some practice and patience, you will be amazed at what you can learn to fold in just one weekend.

Paper folding is a highly rewarding craft that you can do anywhere at any time and which yields relatively quick results. There are no age limitations and next to no cost (depending on which paper you use). Many people have found that it reduces stress, promotes relaxation, develops mental concentration and boosts their overall creativity.

Once you have learnt a few basic folding skills, the possibilities are limitless – the slightest variation in angle of fold or measurement will dramatically change the final outcome and therein lies the excitement. There is always a new structure to discover and once you start, I promise you will want to keep exploring to see what designs of your own you can create next.

This book will introduce you to some basic folding skills and guide you through the process of making a collection of eight beautiful and functional products. As you work through the projects, the techniques will gradually increase in complexity and, on completion, you will be fully equipped with the skills, knowledge and confidence to experiment and design your own unique pieces.

You might explore this wonderful craft for a single weekend, or it could become the start of something bigger. Wherever it takes you, I hope you find it inspiring and enjoyable.

Happy folding!

WORKING WITH PAPER

Paper is a wonderfully versatile material and can be sourced just about anywhere in the world. It is clean, flexible, easy to work with and relatively inexpensive. The more you work with it, the more you will appreciate its quirks, the way the different textures and brands feel, the range of beautiful colours available and how it reacts to being folded.

Choosing paper

You will quickly learn to enjoy the process of selecting papers for specific projects depending on their scale and design and, as your appreciation and confidence in working with it grows, you will find yourself exploring a host of new creative possibilities.

You can begin folding with basic cartridge or brown kraft paper and, when you feel ready, you can delve into the huge array of more luxurious textured, marbled and pattered varieties. They all have different qualities, which you will quickly become acquainted with once you start to work with them.

The thickness of paper you use is crucial and must be considered at the start of every project. Too light and it can lack strength, too heavy and the folds will crack. Visualize some tissue paper, a sheet of printer paper and a piece of cardboard. You can immediately see how you might be able to fold with one but not with another. Each has unique qualities: thin paper can be folded into many layers without becoming too bulky, whereas thicker paper will be stronger but can be difficult to crease into small patterns.

Paper weight

The thickness or density of paper is measured by its grams per square metre (gsm), or grammage. This is calculated by the amount a sheet of paper would weigh in grams if it was exactly one square metre in size. For example, if you have a 120gsm paper that is 1×1 metre in size, it would weigh 120 grams. The higher the number, the thicker the paper will be. This system is used very widely internationally but in North America and parts of Latin America you may find paper weight categorized by its basis weight (see page 79 for more details).

A rough guide to different weights of paper:

80–100gsm	Thin (standard copier paper)
100–120gsm	Medium-weight paper
120–160gsm	Thick paper
160–200gsm	Thin card
200–300gsm	Medium-weight card
300+ gsm	Thick card

In this book we use papers ranging from 100–270gsm, depending on the size of project. The smaller, more intricate projects require a lighter weight of paper and the larger ones, a slightly heavier one. At the start of each project there is a recommended weight of paper for you to source. This is a rough guide only and it is well worth experimenting to see what works best for you and your projects.

Paper sizes

I usually purchase the largest sheets of paper I can find and then cut them to the required measurements. This limits waste and is more cost effective. However, depending on the available space you have and what you feel most comfortable with, you may wish to buy several smaller-sized sheets and join the separate pieces together.

Choosing colour

You may choose to work exclusively in white, which will emphasize the light and the shadows in your folded pieces. However, part of the joy of working with paper is the availability of a spectrum of colours, so why not use them? Even just one colour, or a combination of two or more, will give your work a unique appeal and make it instantly recognizable.

There are many books, and lots of information available online about colour theory that can help you select colour palettes. However, you can also find inspiration all around you – get into the habit of taking a quick photograph or making a note of the combinations you see that work well or you particularly like. These can then be applied to your folding projects.

Using patterned paper

Introducing pattern can dramatically change the appearance of your work. It's advisable to be cautious as very busy patterns may affect the visibility of the folds – the light, shadow and folded planes could become less obvious. However, folds can distort patterns in interesting ways and make your projects even more unique. If you want to use pattern, but don't want it to dominate or distract, try using just one section as an accent and leave the rest in a plain colour.

You can buy beautiful patterned papers from specialist paper stores (see page 80). But before going shopping, why not try repurposing what you already have? Try rescuing old printed letters destined for the recycling bin, manuscripts, unused wallpaper, maps, calendars or even sheet music you no longer use.

Be mindful of the weight and texture of the paper; if it is too thin or old, it may not fold particularly well and textured handmade papers can be too thick. Shiny wrapping paper and magazine pages should also be avoided as they tend to crack along the fold lines. Don't let this put you off though – experiment with whatever you have and the results may surprise you.

MATERIALS

You don't need many tools to get started: at its simplest, just the paper itself and your hands. However, a few select tools will make the process easier and give you more options. You many already have some of them at home and, if not, most can be found in art supply or stationery shops.

HOLE PUNCH

SHORT RULER

BONE FOLDER

LONG RULER

SCORING TOOL

PENCIL

DOUBLE-SIDED TAPE,
10MM (³/₈IN) WIDE

ERASER

CRAFT KNIFE AND
SPARE BLADES

1MM (^{1}/$_{16}$IN) STRING OR WAX-COVERED COTTON

SHARPENER

SCISSORS

SELF-HEALING CUTTING MAT

PAPER IN VARIOUS COLOURS
AND WEIGHTS

PREPARING THE PAPER

Once you have selected which colour and weight of paper to use you will need to cut it to the required size (and apply double-sided tape if required). This part can be quite laborious but try to see it as part of the process and something to be done to perfection to get you off to a good start.

Cutting the paper to size

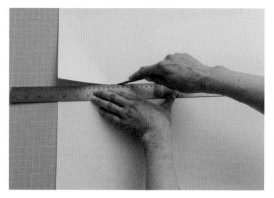

Each project in this book gives a specific size of paper and it will need to be measured and cut exactly. Measure and mark cutting points along one edge of the paper lightly with a pencil, or make an indentation with the scoring tool. With the paper on a self-healing cutting mat on a flat surface, align the ruler carefully with the marks and firmly cut with a craft knife, leaning it against the metal edge of the ruler. Use a safety ruler if possible and work very carefully.

Using a scoring tool

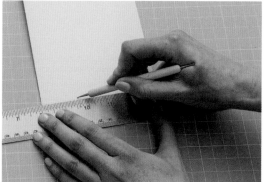

The purpose of scoring is to make an indentation or dent along the line you will be folding. The score must never cut through the paper. No matter what kind of scoring tool you use: the point of a bone folder, a stylus dotting tool (as pictured), the blunt side of a craft knife or a ballpoint pen that has run out of ink, the scoring method is the same.

Place the ruler down on the paper where you want to score and run the tool along the edge of the ruler. With practice, you will learn how firmly to draw the line so you achieve the depth and pressure of score you want.

Tape allowance

When making the projects in this book it is **very important** to remember that the tape allowance is additional to the measurements given for the length of paper and is included in the number shown in square brackets. Never include this area in your calculations or measurements for scoring. Cut your paper using the larger number. If in doubt, you can cut it wider than you need and trim it down to size after you have applied the tape. I recommend you use double-sided tape 10mm (⅜in) wide.

Adding double-sided tape to edges

Many projects require either separate pieces of paper or two ends of the same piece to be stuck together. You may need to join different types of paper (e.g. a different colour or pattern) together at the start or during the steps of a project. You can use glue or any kind of adhesive but my preference is to use double-sided tape as it is less messy, much easier to use and can be pre-prepared.

Take a piece of tape slightly longer than you will need and carefully place it along the short edge of the paper, as instructed. You can then trim off any excess tape with a craft knife. It can take a bit of practice before you are able to place the tape accurately. Score along the inner edge so it will be easy to fold over when required. Do not remove the other side of the backing until you are about to stick the edges together.

Joining edges

When the instructions tell you to stick edges together, peel off the backing and place the untaped edge on top of the sticky one to make the join almost unnoticeable and flat on both sides. Do not 'hem' the join, i.e. stick two edges together as you would with fabric, as this will create an extra flap on the back of the piece and upset your measurements.

In the project instructions the front side of the paper is the side with the tape facing you. The back side is the side where you cannot see the tape.

DIVIDING THE PAPER

Dividing paper is an important principle in paper folding and it is vital you learn how to do it accurately. The majority of projects in this book start by making equal linear divisions and there are two methods: by hand or using a ruler and scoring tool. Both techniques are shown here but, for consistency, all the projects in this book will use the scoring method below.

Scoring-tool method

This method is more suitable for heavier types of paper and larger projects. You will also achieve a more defined fold on heavier paper if you score it first.

1. Measure and mark Using a ruler and a pencil, make marks along the top and bottom edges of the sheet of paper at equal spaces apart, according to the width of divisions you need.

2. Score the lines Place your ruler flat on the sheet and align it to the pencil marks on both sides. Leaning against the ruler, firmly score along each line with a scoring tool.

3. Final stage The sheet is now divided into equal sections. Most of the projects in this book begin with this process and give the measurements you need to divide each piece by.

Folding method

This method allows for the equal division of paper into halves, quarters, eighths (shown below), and so on. It is most suitable for lighter weights of paper.

1. Fold in half Take the lower edge of the paper up to meet the opposite edge and fold, dividing it in half. Open it back out flat.

2. Fold into quarters Fold the lower edge up to meet the centre fold, then open out again. Turn the paper and do the same for the opposite outer edge.

3. Quarters are created Open the paper out flat. There should now be four equal sections.

4. Divide the first quarter Take the lower edge up to meet the fold of the first quarter and make a new fold. Then open the paper out flat again.

5. Divide the second quarter This time, take the lower edge to the fold of the third quarter and make a new fold. Flatten the paper out again.

6. Divide the third and fourth quarters Turn the paper around and repeat steps 3 and 4 from the opposite edge, dividing the remaining two quarters.

7. Eighths are created Open out the paper. There are now seven valley folds dividing it into eight equal sections.

FOLDING TECHNIQUES

All folded structures consist of a combination of two basic folds: valley and mountain. It is how they work together and interact with one another that enables a flat sheet of paper to become a simple or complex three-dimensional form. Once you learn a few simple techniques, the possibilities are limitless.

Valley fold

This is the simplest and most basic of all origami or paper folds. Everything you make will start with a valley fold. Fold one edge towards you to meet the opposite edge. When unfolded it will form a 'V' shape.

Mountain fold

A mountain fold is the opposite of a valley fold and can be achieved by simply turning the valley fold over. Alternatively, you can fold one edge away from you to meet the opposite edge.

Universal fold

A universal fold is when the paper is folded in both directions into both a valley and mountain fold. When unfolded, it will lie flat. This means the crease will 'remember' how to fold in either direction when required.

Make your fold one way

Then fold the opposite way

Shaping

As the folding process progresses you will start to
see the magical transformation of a flat sheet into a
three-dimensional form. You will notice that even
a few simple valley folds will cause the sheet to curl
up and curve into itself.

    With more complex patterns, the method of
coaxing the score lines into shape takes a bit of practice.
You will find your own method, but I recommend
placing one hand underneath and the other on the top
and using both hands to gently work along the scored
lines to encourage the paper to find its new form.

Using a bone folder

Using a bone folder is optional but it does give you a
more defined and precise crease. Gently curve the paper
over and, on a flat surface, run the bone folder along the
fold with a swift, smooth motion.

Pre-creasing

While many folds are left in place when we make
them, sometimes we need to fold and unfold.
Make a valley fold and then unfold the paper to
leave the crease. This technique is called making
a pre-crease, since we do not actually use the
crease until later in the folding process.

V fold

This is a highly adaptable and dynamic structure that can be repeated multiple times in all directions and has the ability to make a surface expand and contract. You'll find it used in the Framed artwork (see page 65) and Lotus lampshade (see page 71).

1. Divide in half Fold a sheet of paper in half using a universal fold - a valley and then a mountain going the opposite way (see page 20).

2. Fold the corner With the folded edge on the right, fold the bottom corner diagonally across at a right angle to the other edge.

3. Make it into a universal fold Fold it back in the opposite direction to make it a universal fold.

4. Unfold the paper Open up the paper and you will see a triangular shape. The point in the centre where all four folds meet is called the 'node'.

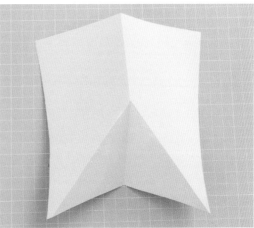

5. Form the shape Squeeze two edges of the triangle together so they become mountain folds and the vertical line above turns into a mountain fold too.

6. Finished shape Each V structure consists of three mountain folds and one valley fold. The central fold changes from a mountain fold to a valley when it crosses the central point or node.

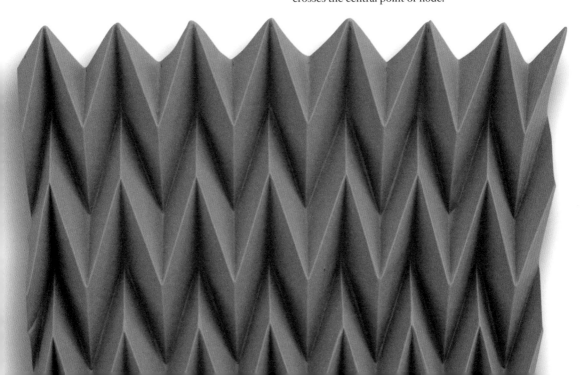

TROUBLESHOOTING

As you work through the projects in this book you will undoubtedly come up against some problems. Don't worry – mistakes are all part of the learning process and are usually easily remedied. Use the tips and problem-solving guide below to help you.

• Practice is key to all paper folding – if your first attempt doesn't work as you'd hoped, don't give up; try again and next time it will be better or you may even create something you hadn't expected to. Remember, making mistakes is all part of the process!

• Fold slowly, methodically and as accurately as you can. Make each score and subsequent fold as precise as possible and try not to rush. No matter how simple the fold, make it a good one.

• Select the right paper for your project – if the instructions recommend a certain weight of paper, try to find one as close as possible. Once you have had some practice you can experiment with different weights, but on your first attempt try to use the recommended type as this will give you the best results.

Problem: The paper splits, or you have cut through it by mistake.
Solution: Apply some invisible tape to the back of the paper and it will look as good as new.

Problem: The paper is cracking along the fold lines or the folds are not as crisp as you'd like.
Solution: The paper is probably too thick for the scale of project you are working on. You can either make this into a feature or start again with a lighter weight of paper.

Problem: I'm not feeling confident about exactly where to score the lines.
Solution: Drawing the score lines in pencil first is highly recommended. It is vital to get the scoring position correct so it's worth taking the time to do this accurately.

Problem: I made a mistake when scoring.
Solution: You can try scoring again in the correct place, but you'll have to be very careful when folding that you fold the correct score. Or you can put this down to experience and start again.

Problem: The paper is losing its rigidity and feeling softer than when I started folding.
Solution: This can easily happen if you are working on the same piece of paper for a long time. Try not to handle the paper too roughly and, as you gain more experience, you'll need to handle the paper less.

Problem: There are marks on the paper and it is not looking as pristine and clean as I had hoped.
Solution: Make sure you always keep your hands and tools clean and try to keep food, drink and pets away from your work surface.

PROJECTS

In the following pages are eight exciting projects that progress in difficulty and build on your skills as you work through them. Try to do them slowly, methodically and in order, if you can. That way, you will learn new techniques to help you make the pieces that follow.

HANGING STAR

This is an easy starter project and it introduces you to some useful basic folding terms and techniques. The star looks attractive from both sides so it works very well as a hanging decoration. It needn't be saved just for the festive season either; made in bright colours, it can make a bold display.

When making this star, you will practise how to equally divide up pieces of paper, a technique that will be used many times through the book. It also demonstrates how valley and mountain folds can work together to create impressive three-dimensional forms.

You can try making it in different sizes, playing around with scale. Be sure to remember to make the proportions the same – 1:4 if using two sheets of paper or 1:8 if you just want to try using one.

Experiment with different papers, or decorate the paper before or after folding. Try making it with patterned papers or using two complementary colours, one for each rectangle.

What you will need

The recommended paper weight for this project is 160–175gsm

*Remember to cut the paper to the longer length shown in square brackets to include the tape allowance. The shorter length is the number you will work with for dividing.

- 2 strips of paper measuring 48[49]* × 12cm (18⅞[19¼]* × 4¾in)

- Double-sided tape, 10mm (⅜in) wide

- Ruler

- Pencil

- Scoring tool

- Hole punch, 3mm (⅛in) is recommended

- 2 lengths of wax-covered cotton, about 30cm (12in)

Hanging star instructions

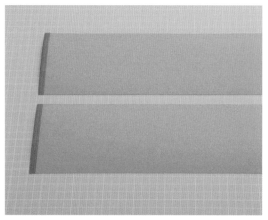

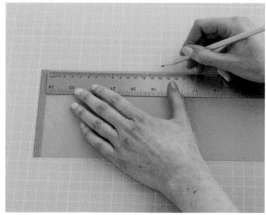

1. Prepare the paper Take the paper and attach double-sided tape to one of the short edges on each piece but do not peel off the backing yet. Score a line along the inner edge of the tape to help with folding it over later in the project.

2. Mark the divisions Working on the front side of the paper (with the tape facing you), divide each piece into eight equal sections of 6cm (2⅜in) each. To do this, use a pencil to make small marks along the top and bottom edges of the paper.

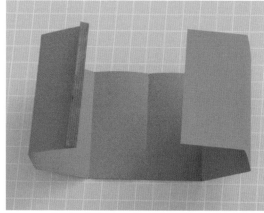

3. Score the divisions Using a scoring tool and ruler, join these marks up with vertical scores so you have eight equal vertical sections.

4. Make valley folds Fold the tape back and then fold each scored line into a valley fold. The paper will curl as you complete them.

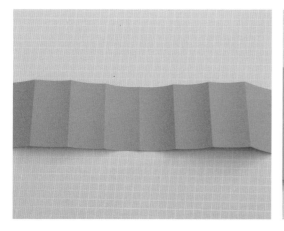

5. Turn it over Turn the paper over so the valley folds now become mountain folds.

6. Fold diagonals Now fold a diagonal line across each pair of vertical sections. You can fold using your hands or score the lines first using a scoring tool and a ruler.

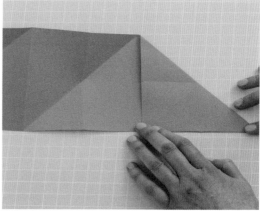

7. Keep going Work along the whole length, folding across two vertical sections each time to make a square.

8. Fold opposite diagonals Keeping the paper on the same side, fold diagonal lines in the opposite direction along the strip of paper so you now have a cross across each of the four squares.

Hanging star continued

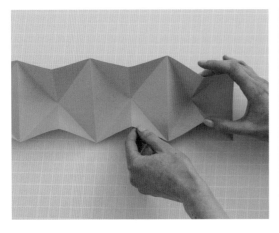

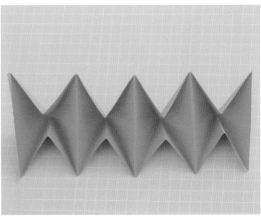

9. Form the shape Pick up the paper and ease the folds gently together so they start to change into a three-dimensional form. Explore how the structure works. You should be able to expand and contract it.

10. Fold another piece Repeat steps 2–9 to make an identical piece using the other strip of paper. Make sure the first valley fold is made on the front side of the sheet, with the tape facing you, and do not include the tape in your folding calculations.

11. Stick two ends together Peel the backing off one of the taped ends and place the non-taped edge of the other piece on top of the sticky part so the join is hardly noticeable.

12. Join to make a circle You should now have one long folded piece. Take the two free ends and, in the same way, stick the remaining taped edge to the non-taped one to create a circular, wreath-like structure.

13. Punch holes Flip the structure inside out so the points are facing upwards. Using a hole punch, place holes in each of the points on the inner part of the circle. Make sure they are roughly in the same place.

14. Thread the string Take a length of string and thread it through each hole, pulling tightly to draw the shape together and form the star. Tie a knot to secure it and trim off the ends.

15. Make a hanging loop Punch another hole at the top, through one of the points, and thread through another length of string to hang the star.

16. Turn it over The star looks different on each side.

ROSETTE

These twisted rosettes, originally created by Paul Jackson, are a versatile and fun decoration that are easy to make. Use them to enhance your gift wrapping, attach to blank card or make a collection to frame as a colourful artwork.

Many folded projects start with straight mountain and valley folds that sit parallel to one another. In this project, the mountain folds are straight parallel lines but the valleys are at an angle creating a zig-zag pattern. The angle of the valley folds allows the structure to be twisted down into a flat two-dimensional form. The top section of the paper is removed so the mountain and valley folds do not meet. Here the edges are secured together after the twisting but this can also be done beforehand by creating a hexagonal tube, which is then twisted down into a flat rosette.

Try experimenting with the measurements and with the proportion of paper you remove. A smaller width will create a hexagonal ring and a half portion will create a different-shaped piece. Some will not lock together without an adhesive, but you will create some interesting forms.

What you will need

The recommended paper weight for this project is 90–100gsm

*Remember to cut the paper to the longer length shown in square brackets to include the tape allowance. The shorter length is the number you will work with for dividing.

- Paper measuring 30[31]* × 10cm (11¾[12¼]* × 4in)
- Double-sided tape, 10mm (⅜in) wide
- Ruler
- Pencil
- Scoring tool
- Craft knife
- Cutting mat

Rosette instructions

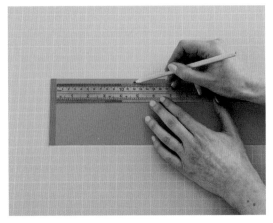

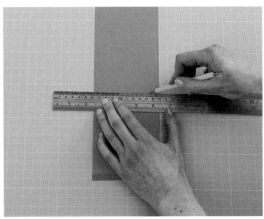

1. Mark measurements Prepare the paper by attaching double-sided tape to one of the short sides. Do not peel off the backing. With the paper placed horizontally and the tape facing up, use a ruler and pencil to lightly mark 6cm (2⅜in) divisions along the top and bottom edges.

2. Score lines Score a line along the inner edge of the tape to help with folding it over later. Rotate the paper so that it is vertical. Use a ruler and scoring tool to score lines between the marks you just made.

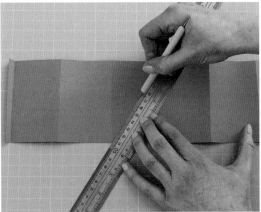

3. Make valley folds At each score line, make a valley fold. As the paper curls, you will see the folds as mountain folds from the other side.

4. Score diagonal lines Lay the paper horizontally in front of you with the mountain folds facing up. Score diagonally in the same direction across each section, from the bottom left corner to the top right corner.

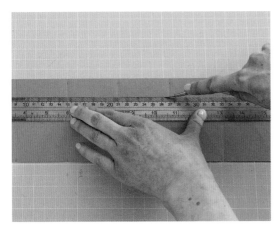

5. Trim off the top edge Use a ruler and craft knife to trim 2.5cm (1in) off the whole of the top edge. This will create the correct angles to work with.

6. Make diagonal valley folds With the mountain folds still facing you, fold the diagonal score lines into valley folds.

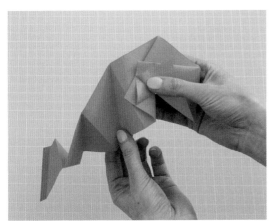

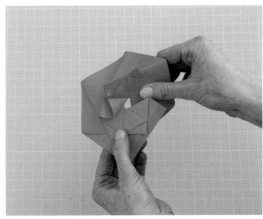

7. Form a circle Gather the paper from the centre, working around to create a twisted, circular shape.

8. Tuck and secure Once you have folded all six sections, peel the backing off the double-sided tape and stick two edges together to secure it.

SPIRAL WIND SPINNER

This spinner makes an attractive and mesmerizing decoration for a window or balcony where you can watch it revolve in the moving air.

Also based on an idea by Paul Jackson, it is made up of a similar structure as the rosette on page 35, using non-parallel lines. Again, the mountain folds will be vertical and parallel while the valley folds remain parallel but have been placed at an angle. The zig-zag pattern can then be gathered up and twisted to make this spiral form. It can also make an attractive two-dimensional flat form or rosette.

    Once you have mastered the technique, try varying the angles of folds and experiment with different shapes of paper such as circular or triangular and you will have some interesting results.

What you will need

The recommended paper weight for this project is 100–120gsm

- Paper measuring 60 × 10cm (23⅝ × 4in)

- Ruler

- Pencil

- Scoring tool

- Hole punch, 3mm (⅛in) is recommended

- String, about 30cm (12in) for hanging

Spiral wind spinner instructions

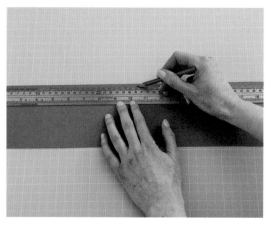

1. Measure and mark Place the paper horizontally in front of you. Using a pencil and ruler, mark 2cm (¾in) spaces along the top and bottom edges.

2. Score lines Rotate the paper so that it is vertical, then use a ruler and scoring tool to score lines between the marks.

3. Create valley folds Fold each scored line into a valley fold.

4. Score diagonal lines Turn the paper over so that the mountain folds are facing up. Score a line diagonally across each section, being careful to angle your line so it is placed a few millimetres away from the vertical mountain fold at the top and bottom of each section and so that the lines do not meet each other.

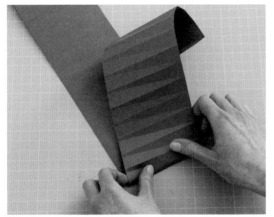

5. Fold the diagonal lines Fold the diagonal scored into valleys. The combination of vertical mountain folds and diagonal valley folds work together to create a spiral form. You will see a beautiful pattern emerge.

6. Gather the folds Gradually gather the folds to create a spiral, circular form.

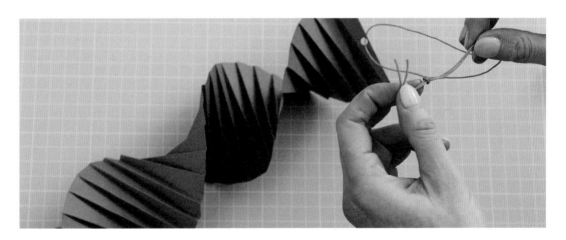

7. Attach string Punch a hole at one end and attach a length of string for hanging.

INTERLOCKING CURVE BALL

These beautiful curved balls are easier to make than they look and are simply constructed from three interlocking strips of paper with curved score lines that simply click into place. They are also sometimes called Triskele paper globes. The origin of their design isn't known.

I have included this project as it is a gentle introduction to the art of curved folding, which is when a fold or scored line is rounded rather than straight. Once mastered, curved folding can produce some beautiful concentric patterns and forms.

A template is provided for this project and each ball will require three pieces. You can either trace over it, photocopy it or use it to cut a template from cardboard that can be used multiple times. You can also try scaling it up to a larger size using a photocopier or by importing it into software. Don't forget to add the 10mm (⅜in) tape allowance to one of the short ends on each piece.

Once you have three templates cut to size, you will need to score the curve with a scoring tool, which can take a bit of practice. If you like, a ribbon or string can be tied under one of the strips before you click it into place, to hang it up. Try using different colours so the individual strips stand out more.

What you will need

The recommended paper weight for this project is 150–270gsm

- Template found on page 45, photocopied or traced three times onto the paper you are using and cut out, adding a 1cm (⅜in) strip for tape on one of the short ends of each piece

- Double-sided tape, 10mm (⅜in) wide

- Pencil

- Tracing paper

- Scoring tool

- Cutting mat

- String or ribbon to hang (optional)

Interlocking curve ball instructions

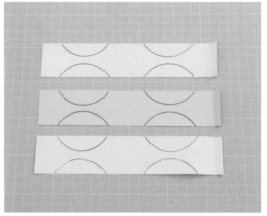

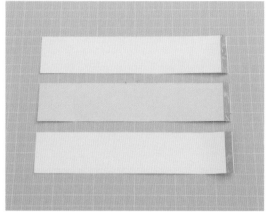

1. Prepare the pieces Either photocopy or trace the template opposite onto the paper you are using, three times. Add 10mm (⅜in) to one end of each piece and then cut them out. The circular marks will be on the back of the pieces.

2. Add the tape Turn over the strips of paper and attach double-sided tape to one of the short sides on each piece. Do not peel off the backing.

3. Score the templates Use a scoring tool to go over the pattern of the template. Repeat for each piece.

4. Form the loops Take one of the strips and peel the top layer off the tape. With the scored pattern on the inside, make a loop by attaching the two ends together. Repeat with a second strip.

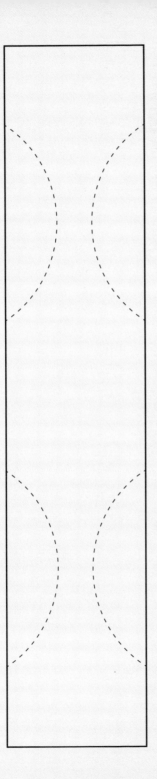

Note

To make bigger or smaller balls, adjust the size of the template by scaling it up or down on a photocopier. Add a 10mm (⅜in) strip at one end of each piece for the tape allowance.

Interlocking curve ball instructions continued

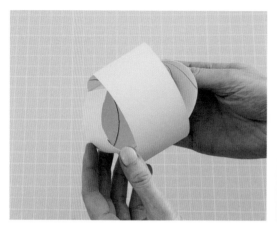

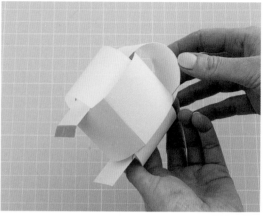

5. Create a ball Place one loop perpendicularly inside the other loop, so that it starts to look like a ball.

6. Insert the third strip Weave the third strip of paper into the other two, going outside the exterior loop and inside the interior loop, as shown.

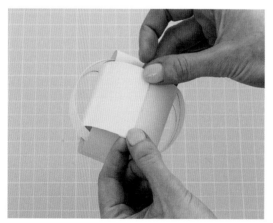

7. Form the last loop Tape the ends of the third strip together, then slide the taped end inside the ball so that it is no longer visible. Adjust each loop to make sure the scored sections are positioned evenly on the outside of the ball.

8. Shape the curves When in position, apply gentle pressure to each of the pre-scored curves so they click into place. Readjust if necessary.

VASE COVER

This surprisingly sturdy piece is very simple to make with just a few simple folds. When a jam jar or glass is placed inside, it makes an unusual way of displaying flowers or storing pencils and make-up brushes. It can even be used as a lantern if you place an LED candle inside (providing the paper you use is light or translucent enough).

The technique is relatively simple and can be adjusted at any stage to produce a completely different structure. Start with a flat sheet of paper, which is scored into equal horizontal divisions on the front side. These are then eased into valley folds so the paper is a curved shape turning inwards. On the back side, vertical guidelines will be drawn and these will be used alongside the horizontal mountain folds as a reference as where to score diagonally.

Try different sizes of paper and experiment with measurements – you could halve the height so you have a shorter structure or extend the length so the circumference will be wider. Alter the spacing of the horizontal divisions or the pencil guidelines on the back. Every small change will result in a completely different finished form. Try using different colours of paper – if you use a grey shade, the piece takes on a convincing ceramic quality from a distance and people are always amazed it is just made from paper.

What you will need

The recommended paper weight for this project is 270gsm

*Remember to cut the paper to the longer length shown in square brackets to include the tape allowance. The shorter length is the number you will work with for dividing.

- Paper measuring 30[31]*cm × 15cm (11¾in[12¼in]* × 6in)

- Double-sided tape, 10mm (⅜in) wide

- Ruler

- Pencil

- Scoring tool

- Eraser

Vase cover instructions

1. Prepare the paper Take the paper and attach double-sided tape to one of the short sides. Do not peel off the backing. Score the inner line of the tape.

2. Measure and mark With the paper placed horizontally and the tape face up, use a ruler and pencil to make marks 3cm (1¼in) apart along the left and right (short) edges.

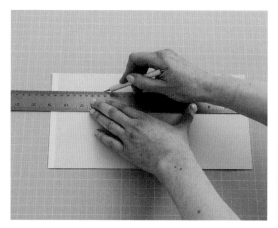

3. Score horizontal lines Use a scoring tool to join the points together, creating five equal horizontal sections.

4. Fold the tape Turn the paper over, then fold the tape back.

5. Draw vertical lines On the back of the paper, use a pencil and ruler to make marks 3cm (1¼in) apart along the top and bottom (long) edges. Draw lines that join the points together.

6. Form valley folds Turn the paper over to the front again. Gently form valley folds along the scored horizontal lines. The folds don't need to be crisp – just aim for a curved form.

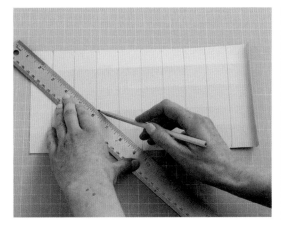

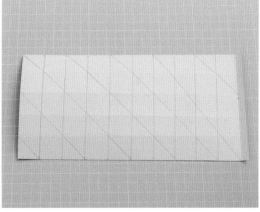

7. Draw diagonal lines, left to right Turn the paper over to the back. Starting in the top left-hand corner, use a pencil and ruler to draw a diagonal line across five columns, making sure you go through the intersection of where the vertical meets the horizontal.

8. Complete the lines Continue drawing lines at the same angle on every second column across the length of the sheet. Remember to go into the corners, too.

Vase cover continued

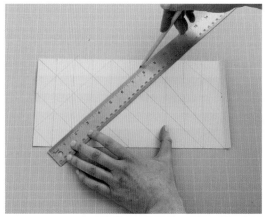

9. Draw diagonal lines, right to left Repeat in the other direction to create a grid of squares. See the diagram opposite for how the finished pattern should look. Carefully check your version against this before you carry on.

10. Score the lines When you are sure you have the correct pattern marked in pencil, score along the diagonal lines in both directions and then erase the pencil lines.

11. Make valley folds from the bottom right Starting at the bottom right corner, fold the diagonal score lines into valley folds.

12. Make valley folds from the top left Move to the top left corner, and create valley folds along the diagonal score lines. You will begin to see the form emerge.

Vase cover folding pattern diagram

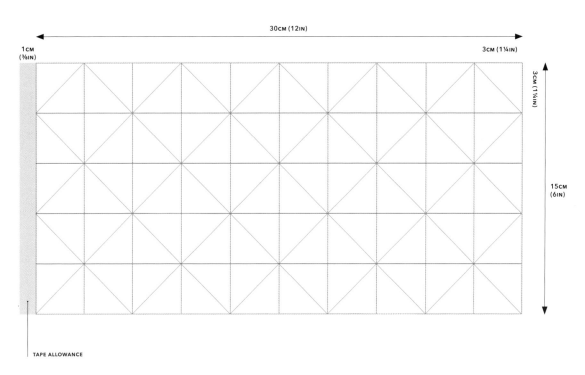

30CM (12IN)

1CM (⅜IN)

3CM (1¼IN)

3CM (1¼IN)

15CM (6IN)

TAPE ALLOWANCE

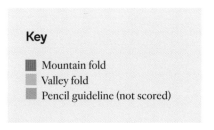

Key

Mountain fold
Valley fold
Pencil guideline (not scored)

Vase cover continued

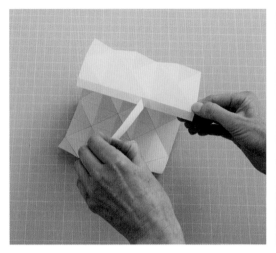

13. Create a rounded shape Gently ease the paper into a circular form, then remove the backing of the double-sided tape.

14. Join the sides Use the tape to join the short sides together, making sure to match all the folds and angles.

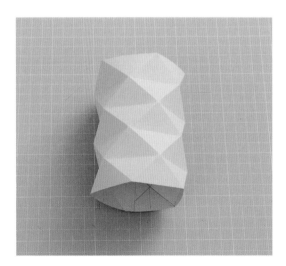

15. Finished piece It is now ready for a jam jar to be placed inside.

BAUBLE

Paper baubles are one of the most popular and fun things you can fold. They make fantastic presents and once you learn the basic technique, you'll discover that there are infinite variations, sizes and forms that you can create. You will soon find your favourite design and remember, they're not just for Christmas.

The bauble is made from a length of paper equally divided vertically on the front side using valley folds. Horizontal guidelines are then drawn in pencil on the back side and used along with the existing mountain folds as a reference for where to score the diagonal lines.

The slightest variation from the size of paper you start with, the width of divisions or the spacing of the guidelines will change the final outcome and you will have a completely different form. It's highly addictive! Try experimenting with scale, different papers, colours and patterns and you will soon build up a large and varied collection.

What you will need

The recommended paper weight for this project is 160gsm

*Remember to cut the paper to the longer length shown in square brackets to include the tape allowance. The shorter length is the number you will work with for dividing.

- Paper measuring 36[37]* × 14cm (14⅛[14½]* × 5½in)

- Double-sided tape, 10mm (⅜in) wide

- Ruler

- Scoring tool

- Pencil

- Hole punch, 3mm (⅛in) is recommended

- String, about 30cm (12in)

Bauble instructions

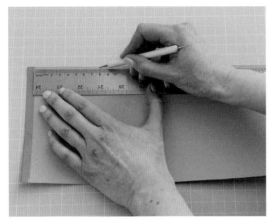

1. Make indentations Take the paper and attach double-sided tape to one of the short sides. Do not peel off the backing. With the paper horizontal and the tape face up, use a ruler and scoring tool to make indentations 2cm (¾in) apart along the top and bottom.

2. Score lines Rotate the paper so that it is vertical and score lines by joining up the indentations.

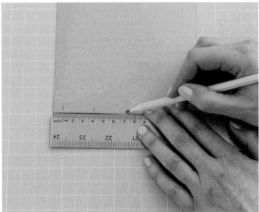

3. Mark measurements Turn the paper over and, with a pencil and ruler, mark the following measurements along the top and bottom (short) edges: 1cm (⅜in), 4cm (1½in), 7cm (2¾in), 10cm (4in) and 13cm (5⅛in).

4. Draw horizontal lines Turn the paper so that it is horizontally in front of you and, with a pencil and ruler, draw lines, joining up the marks you just made. You will have a 1cm (⅜in) space at the top and bottom and the remaining space will be divided into three.

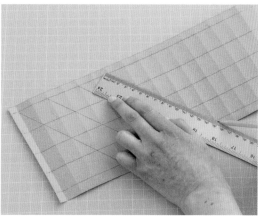

5. Make valley folds Turn the sheet over to the front again. Fold the tape towards the back, then make a valley fold along each scored line.

6. Draw diagonal lines, left to right Lay the paper flat with the mountain folds facing up. Starting in the top left corner, just below your first pencil line, draw a diagonal line across four folds. Finish at the bottom pencil line. Continue until you reach the end of the paper.

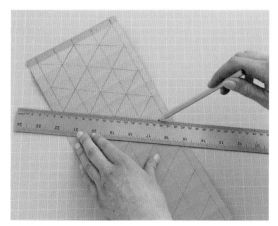

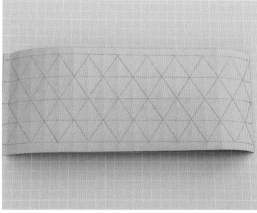

7. Draw diagonal lines, right to left Repeat in the other direction to form a diamond pattern.

8. Complete the diamond pattern The final pattern should look like this. Refer to the diagram on page 60 to carefully check your pattern is correct. Make any adjustments needed before you continue.

Bauble folding pattern diagram

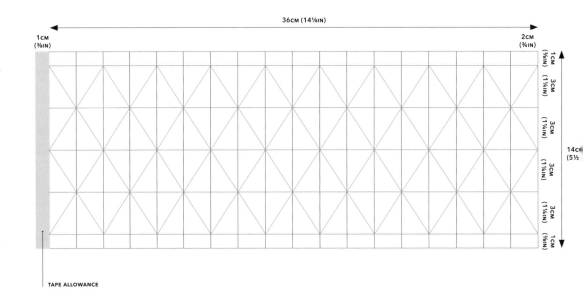

36CM (14⅛IN)

1CM
(⅜IN)

2CM
(¾IN)

1CM (⅜IN)
3CM (1¼IN)
3CM (1¼IN)
3CM (1¼IN)
3CM (1¼IN)
1CM (⅜IN)

14CM
(5½

TAPE ALLOWANCE

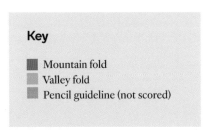

Key

Mountain fold
Valley fold
Pencil guideline (not scored)

9. Score the diagonal lines Now score the diagonal lines in both directions. Try to stop before you reach the top and bottom 1cm (⅜in) strips, but it doesn't matter if you do go all the way to the edge.

10. Create valley folds, right to left Working from right to left, create valley folds along the diagonal scored lines.

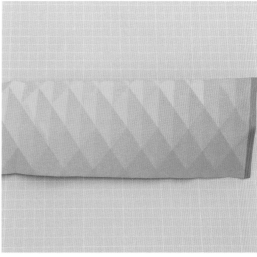

11. Create valley folds, left to right Repeat, but this time work from left to right.

12. The form takes shape You should now see the three-dimensional form that is beginning to take shape.

Bauble continued

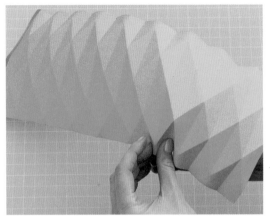

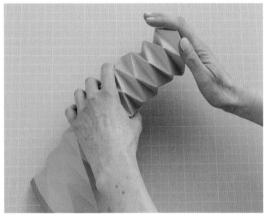

13. Gather the outer folds Start to create the form by encouraging the outer edges to come together. This takes a bit of practice.

14. Compress the folds Encourage the form to concertina by gently compressing the folds.

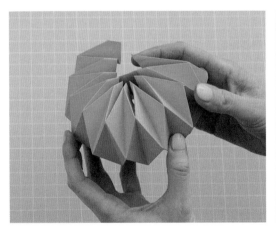

15. Bring the ends together You should now be able to curve the form around, bringing the two ends together, so that a ball is formed.

16. Punch holes Using a hole punch, pierce a hole in each point on the inner part of the circle.

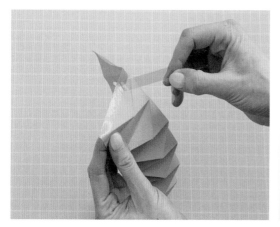

17. Prepare the tape Peel the top layer off the tape.

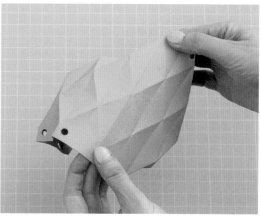

18. Attach the ends Secure the two ends together by placing the untaped end over the taped end. Try to match all the folds as accurately as you can.

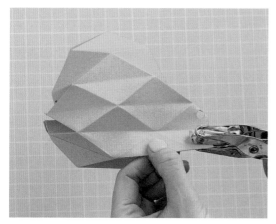

19. Re-punch a hole Where the two ends meet, you will need to re-punch a hole.

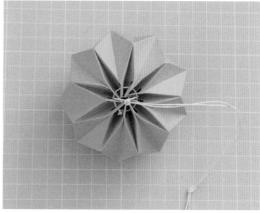

20. Shape, then thread string Reshape the sphere, then thread string through the holes. To attach the piece of hanging string, lay it across the opening underneath the other string. Pull tight, secure with a knot and the hanging string will be securely attached. Trim off any extra string.

FRAMED ARTWORK

By now you will have noticed how beautiful the folded form is, whether it has a function or not. To celebrate this, you can mount or frame your work for it to be admired. It also makes a wonderful gift.

As your piece will be three dimensional, you will need a box frame with enough depth to allow for the height of the piece; this one was 5cm (2in) deep. You can mount any folded work you want – even if it is simple, it can still be an artwork.

For this piece, you will be introduced to a well-known zig-zag structure (also known as the Miura-ori or Herringbone tessellation) consisting of multiple V folds (see page 22) that are made up of valley, mountain and universal folds (see page 20), and can be expanded and contracted to fold flat. There are methods of creating this pattern entirely by hand, but for this project we will use thicker paper that requires scoring.

This technique is quite time consuming as you must score the alternate lines of folds on the front side as well as the back; however, it is worthwhile as it will make the folding of the finished form much easier.

Once you have mastered the techniques, you will be ready to experiment with an infinite number of new designs. Try using a range of colours or different types of paper, such as patterned or something personal, like a map of a place that means something to you or a loved one. You can also play with the colour of mount board. Experiment with different measurements, too. The slightest alteration in the width of divisions or the angle of the folds will completely change the finished piece.

What you will need

The recommended paper weight for this project is 160gsm

- Paper measuring 45 × 20cm (17¾ × 7⅞in)

- Ruler

- Pencil

- Scoring tool

- Mount board, cut to the inner dimensions of the frame

- Glue gun

- Box frame with inner dimensions of 24.5 × 24.5 × 5cm (9¾ × 9¾ × 2in) and outer dimensions of 27 × 27 × 6.5cm (10½ × 10½ × 2⅝in)

Framed artwork instructions

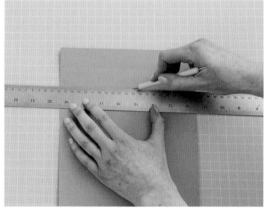

1. Measure and mark Place the paper horizontally in front of you. Use a ruler and pencil, make marks 3cm (1¼in) apart along the top and bottom edges.

2. Score lines Turn the paper around so that it is vertical. Using the marks as a guide, score the paper into 3cm (1¼in) divisions across the width.

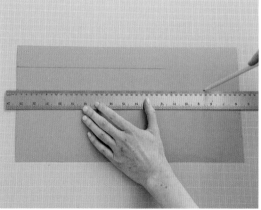

3. Mark measurements on the back Turn the paper over and use a ruler and pencil to mark points at the top and bottom, 4cm (1½in) apart.

4. Draw guidelines Using the points as a reference, draw guidelines 4cm (1½in) apart along the length.

5. Make valley folds Turn the paper over to the front again and form the first set of score lines you made into valley folds.

6. Create universal folds You are now going to turn the valley folds into universal folds. Do this by turning the paper over to the back and folding the mountain folds into valleys. The paper should lie flat instead of being curved.

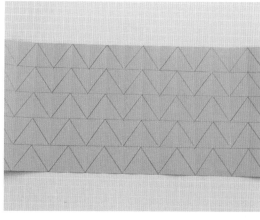

7. Draw V shapes With the back of the paper still facing you, use the folds and pencil lines as guides to draw V shapes, as shown.

8. Complete the pattern Continue until you have drawn V shapes across the entire length of paper.

Framed artwork continued

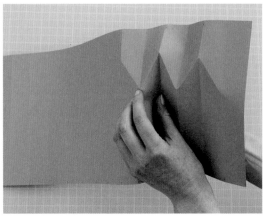

9. Score the diagonal lines When you are happy with the pattern, use a short ruler and a scoring tool to score each diagonal line.

10. Manipulate the V shapes Turn the paper over and work on the front side. With one hand underneath the paper and the other above, slowly manipulate the paper until the V shapes become visible.

11. Identify the lines to re-score Once the pattern is visible but not folded, you will need to re-score every alternate horizontal line of the V shapes. In this case, it is the second and fourth ones from the top.

12. Re-score the lines Work your way along these lines, re-scoring on the front side.

13. Compress the folds The paper is now ready to fold. This step takes a bit of practice, but keep in mind the form you are aiming for and refer back to page 64 at any time. Keep one hand underneath and slowly compress the folds, letting the structure take shape.

14. Contract the paper When you have folded the paper, start to contract it – this will make the folds more defined.

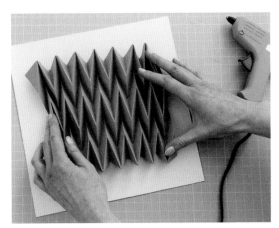

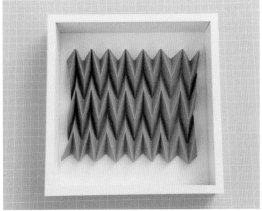

15. Secure to the mount board To securely attach it to the mount board, use a hot glue gun and apply glue to as many contact points as possible.

16. Frame and hang Place the board inside the frame and hang it in a prominent place.

LOTUS LAMPSHADE

This lampshade is the culmination of everything you have learnt so far in this book. By now you should be feeling quite confident in working with paper as a base material. You have folded different weights and hopefully will be able to work with a larger size of paper. Like all the other projects, these instructions and measurements are simply a guide. Once you feel confident with the techniques you can experiment and create your own unique forms.

Be creative with the colours you choose for your shade. As it is open at the bottom, most of the light will be emitted downwards, so it is not essential to use a translucent or white paper.

    You will need either one long piece of paper (wallpaper works well, for instance) or several pieces joined together, so make sure you have plenty of space to work. If you choose the first option, this shade can be made with one long piece measuring: 120[121]* × 34cm (47¼[47⅝]* × 13⅜in). But if you would like to make the same version as pictured, with coloured sections spliced in, prepare the four separate sizes listed opposite.

What you will need

The recommended paper weight for this project is 270gsm

*Remember to cut the paper to the longer length shown in square brackets to include the tape allowance. The shorter length is the number you will work with for dividing.

• To replicate the shade shown here, prepare 4 pieces

COLOURED PAPER:
34 × 10cm (13⅜ × 4in)
34 × 20cm (13⅜in × 7⅞in)

WHITE PAPER:
34 × 30[32]*cm (13⅜in × 12[12⅝]*in)
34 × 60[62]*cm (13⅜in × 23⅝[24½]*in)

• Heat-resistant double-sided tape, 10mm (⅜in) wide

• Long metal ruler

• Pencil

• Scoring tool

• Short ruler

• Eraser

• Hole punch, 3mm (⅛in) is recommended

• String or waxed cotton, about 30cm (12in)

• Cord lock (optional)

Safety

Use an LED light bulb, with a maximum of 10 watts, so that the shade won't get too hot. You can also spray the inside of the shade with specialist fire-proofing spray.

Lampshade instructions

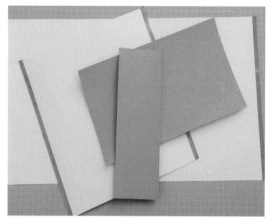

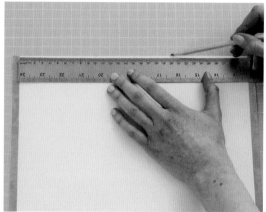

1. Prepare the paper Attach double-sided tape to the 34cm (13⅜in) sides of both white pieces. If you are using one long sheet of paper, attach tape to one short side. Do not peel the backing off the tape.

2. Mark measurements Take one of the pieces of paper and place it horizontally in front of you. Using a ruler and pencil, make a mark every 5cm (2in) along the top and bottom edges. Repeat for each piece.

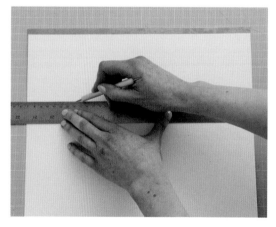

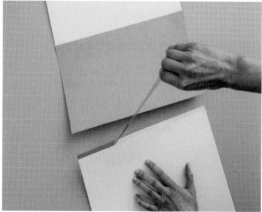

3. Score lines Rotate the paper so that it is vertical. Using a ruler and scoring tool, score lines by joining up the marks. Repeat for each piece.

4. Join the sheets Use the tape to join all the pieces together to make one sheet.

5. Join the sheets continued You should be left with a strip of tape at just one end.

6. Mark measurements Turn the paper over to the back. With it placed horizontally and, working from the top edge, use a ruler and pencil to mark the following measurements at both ends and in the mid-way: 14cm (5½in), 18cm (7in), 21cm (8¼in) and 24cm (9½in).

7. Draw lines Using the longest ruler you have, draw horizontal lines by joining up all the marks.

8. Fold over the tape Fold the double-sided tape towards you.

Lampshade continued

9. Create valley folds Turn the sheet over to the front and form valley folds from the scored lines you made in Step 3.

10. Fold the paper divisions Carefully fold the divisions where two sheets have been attached.

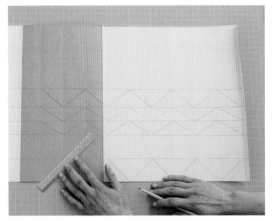

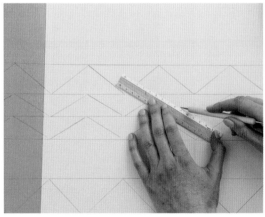

11. Draw a V-shaped pattern Turn the paper over to the back again. Use the valley folds you just made (now mountain folds) and the horizontal pencil lines as guides to help you draw V shapes. There will be a row of three V shapes, followed by an empty row and a further row of V shapes at the bottom.

12. Score the V shapes Once you have marked out the design in pencil, use a scoring tool to go over the lines.

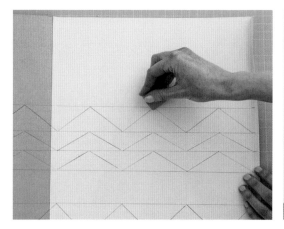

13. Erase the pencil lines When you are happy with the scored lines, use an eraser to remover the pencil guidelines (unless you want them to be visible inside the finished shade).

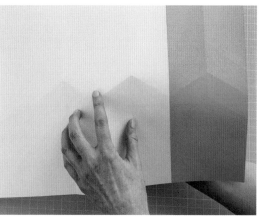

14. Gently ease the V shapes Turn the paper over to the front and with one hand underneath and the other on the front, ease the scored lines so that they're visible.

15. Re-score the middle V shapes Once you can clearly see the V shapes, re-score the middle V shape on the front side of the paper to make the process of folding easier.

16. Fold the V shapes Gradually and carefully fold the scored V shapes, working your way across the length and back again as many times as you need to.

Lampshade continued

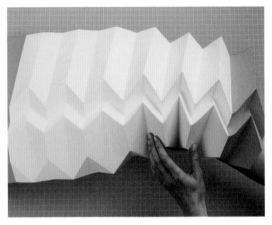

17. The shade begins to take shape Eventually the structure will emerge.

18. Gather the folds Gather the shade as best you can, like a concertina – this takes a bit of practice.

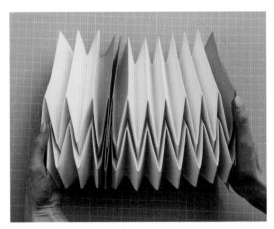

19. Compress the shade You should now be able to compress and contract it completely, making the folds crisp and defined.

20. Punch holes Now turn the paper over to the back – this will be the interior of the shade. At the end of each valley fold, use a hole punch to create holes along the length of the shade.

21. Prepare the tape Remove the top layer from the double-sided tape.

22. Attach the two ends Bring the untaped end around and place it on top of the sticky edge, matching up all the V folds as best as you can.

23. Thread string Thread a length of string or wax-covered cotton through the punched holes.

24. Secure and hang Secure the string with a knot or preferably a cord lock. To hang the shade, loosen the string and place it over the bulb holder and bulb. Pull the string tight so it is secured around the lighting wire and the shade is supported by the bulb holder.

Basis weight

There are two conventions currently in widespread use for paper weights. In Europe and most parts of the world we use ISO paper sizes, which are weighed in grams per square metre (gsm or grammage, see page 9). In the US, Canada and parts of Mexico an older convention is used where the weight of a 500-sheet ream of paper in its uncut form, usually specified in pounds (lb), is known as the basis weight of the paper.

There are many different types of uncut paper, including bond, text/book, cover, index and tag. As there is no standard size for uncut paper, it can be hard to compare different weights and characteristics. Higher values do not necessarily correspond to a heavier paper like they do with gsm, and two papers may share the same basis weight but have very different characteristics. For this reason, it is often necessary to list a metric measurement alongside the US basis weight. The list below should help you identify the basis weight for the sizes of paper used in this book.

Bond (office paper)
Common uses: office copiers, printers and letterheads.
Weights for paper sized: 558.8 x 431.8mm (22 x 17in)

gsm	basis weight
75gsm	20lb (very similar to 80gsm A4 office paper)
90gsm	24lb
120gsm	32lb
135gsm	36lb

Tag (durable strong paper)
Common uses: print tags and labels.
Weights for paper sized: 914.4 x 609.6mm (36 x 24in)

gsm	basis weight
55gsm	34lb
57gsm	35lb

Cover (light card)
Common uses: business cards, invitations and postcards.
Weights for paper sized: 660.4 x 508mm (26 x 20in)

gsm	basis weight
135gsm	50lb
163gsm	60lb
176gsm	65lb
216gsm	80lb
243gsm	90lb
271gsm	100lb

Index (stiff paper)
Common uses: index cards, postcards and sketchbooks.
Weights for paper sized: 774.7 x 647.7mm (30½ x 25½in)

gsm	basis weight
163gsm	90lb
203gsm	110lb
252gsm	140lb

Text/Book (light paper)
Common uses: books, booklets, catalogues and magazines.
Weights for paper sized: 965.2 x 635mm (38 x 25in)

gsm	basis weight
104gsm	70lb
118gsm	80lb
133gsm	90lb
148gsm	100lb
178gsm	120lb

Note on measurements

The imperial measurements in this book have been converted from metric. Never mix imperial and metric measurements.

Suppliers

Paper

G. F Smith: gfsmith.com
Ola Studio: olastudio.co.uk
Shepherds: store.bookbinding.co.uk

Art supplies

Jackson's Art Supplies: jacksonsart.com
Fred Aldous: fredaldous.co.uk
Hobbycraft: hobbycraft.co.uk

Lighting supplies

Dannells: dannells.com
Creative Cables: creative-cables.co.uk

Further reading

Folding Techniques for Designers Second Edition: From Sheet to Form by Paul Jackson (Laurence King, 2022)

Complete Pleats: Pleating Techniques for Fashion Architecture and Design by Paul Jackson (Laurence King, 2015)

Paper Sculpture: Fluid Forms by Richard Sweeney (Schiffer, 2021)

About the author

Kate Colin is a paper-folding artist and designer based in Glasgow. Inspired by origami and geometric form, Kate creates modern, handcrafted lighting designs and other products for interiors, retail, individual clients and brands including Prada and Burberry. Her work has been featured in the *Financial Times*, *Elle Decoration*, *Living*, *Homes & Interiors*, *Country Living* and *Stylist*. She teaches students at all levels, hosts regular online and in-person workshops and has created a course for Domestika.

katecolindesign.com
Follow on Instagram: @kate_colin_design

Acknowledgements

Special thanks to G. F Smith for supplying the paper and Paul Jackson, whose work continues to inform and inspire. Virginia and Zara at Skittledog for calmly and patiently guiding me through this process and Charlie for capturing my work so beautifully.

Finally, to Scott and Clara for your daily support and encouragement.